Protection
From Erasure

SAMI MIRANDA

JADED IBIS PRESS

Published by Jaded Ibis Press
A nonprofit, feminist press publishing socially engaged literature jadedibispress.com

Cover design by Crystal J. Hairston

Trade Paperback ISBN: 978-1-938841-04-0
eBook ISBN: 978-1-938841-13-2
Advanced Copy: 2022 Printed and bound in the United States of America.

Contents

Protection
From Erasure
SAMI MIRANDA

Self Portrait with Mullet at 120 Pounds Soaking Wet

● ● ●

This is an unfamiliar space,
one where I am the unfamiliar.

They notice the difference
I know who is different.

I look for those who know
where I am from,

who know empty pockets
don't translate to empty

minds. Can't wrap my mind around
how home is a different something,

how family questions my belonging,
how they want to wash away the unfamiliar.

Fuck it, I'm just listening
to music that will move my feet,

see if unfamiliar becomes enticing
enough, for someone to want

to dance with me.

Metamorphosis

● ● ●

We are all cocoons,
inside us, a metamorphosis
awakened, it
causes migration to
become need
drives the wings
out of our shoulder blades
and lightens our bones.

Flight, new to us
is like swimming in rough water.

Landing
is always
a roll of the dice,
so we stay in the air
displaced, unsure and tiring, ever tiring,

easy targets for boys
with nets and pins,
who see us as things
to capture
not knowing our need.

Not caring that our destination
The place our hearts guide us to
Is not here, not this place.

ILL Legal

After Sajal Sarkar

● ● ●

You are no longer
this place. No longer accepted.
Uprooted. The tree removed
from the landscape, beauty
no longer found in your flower,
comfort no longer found in your shade.

What does it mean
to be home –
less? A human
is borderless
until a line is drawn
into the dirt that houses the bones
and then they become
not man, not woman
but flag,
a thing to be defined
by the imagination
of limited minds.

What does it mean to be told
you are, or are not
of a place
you have always been from,
not from a dirt that knows your blood
not from a place whose soil is fertilized
with your ancestors,

that you must flee the home
that once held you to its chest.

Home

Poem composed from phrases and words
cut from *National Geographic* magazines

● ● ●

When it's time to leave it all behind:
    discard, button, bead, or bauble
    leave all things unfamiliar
    be sure not to miss the boat.

People are moving, quietly
migratory water birds in flight.
Many immigrants land
in a city of so many places, everyone
sooner or later finds one special
they name, home.

Strong Currents Bring Us Here

*"En un bote de vela, a la mar me tiro Que
me lleve el viento, muy lejos contigo"*
"Botecito de Vela" - La Sonora
Santanera

● ● ●

We came to this,
at times driven into the smell of salt water
by the sting of whip and the bonds of chains,
at times escaping into the smell of salt water
when need combined with the myth of better
made it necessary.
Wind against sail, and wave against wood
now making decisions our feet once made,
taking us farther than the roads
that calloused our bare feet
and wore away at the soles of our shoes ever did.

Sometimes we rode the ocean
sin rumbo fijo
like mangrove seedlings,
flat and fast
turning vertical only when we found ourselves
in brackish water,
knowing here was where our roots
would need to take hold.

Strong currents brought us here
and this will become home now
a place where floating

is the natural state of things,
until our feet find their footing
or sink into sand too soft to hold our weight.

We have not come here alone.
We bring ancestors
who have passed down
the medicine of memory.
We know roots that drink
from fresh water
we are ceiba
anchored on earth but touching sky.
We are also mangrove
growing where land and water meet,
bearing the brunt of ocean-borne storms and hurri-
canes,
finding breath where most
would drown.

"Que me lleve el viento, muy lejos contigo
En un bote de vela, sin marca y compás"
        "Botecito de Vela" - La Sonora Santanera

Anthropology of a Crowd

After Obayya Puttur

● ● ●

Here,
you are
a single entity,
a protagonist
who understands
you are not alone
but part of a crowd,
one brick in a foundation.

Here, you understand who you are,
that your role is to be
one in many, converging
into a mass
that the opportunity
to be just one
is built on.

Phantom in the Museum
of the Americas

● ● ●

In the museum, Phantom
cries, knows

the objects he sees
don't belong here,

delivered to this place
by sword and cross.

The rooster in him wants to crow
a sadness, that wakes spirits.

Instead, he mixes colors,
creates images,
sings stories
stolen from his ears,
but always in his hands.

Protection from Predators

Poem composed from phrases and words
cut from *National Geographic* magazines

● ● ●

A young man asks his father why
Blacks born in the United States
feel unwelcome,
"Ask one of the Americans who've survived."

Oh lord, won't you buy me …
protection from predators,
armor against decay.

Listen, this is tough to admit;
time has not eased
the grief of a woman
whose son died.

Prayer softens hard times for families.
I would like to think that,
But no.

One day I called on Nina,
she still smelled of charred flesh
raising a hymn on Sunday,
barbed but beautiful.
This song should be sung only by its owners.

This America

● ● ●

This America
is not new,
is rooted in earth
invaded by feet shod
in biblical inconsistencies.
        (just call them lies)
Has grown on bodies
buried after flame has already
taken care of decomposition,
after sword, and pistol, and noose.
        (everything was a weapon in search of genocide)

No, this America
is not new.
It has kicked at the pregnant belly
of equality until it bled out
its fruit.
        (who wants a child that understands its right to
rebellion anyway)
It has shackled tongue
until language leaves it
replaced it with an unfamiliar vocabulary
forced to express ideas it can't contain.
        (they handicap our truth, or it would cut them
down)

No, this America

is not new.
It has always built
walls around itself, separating
difference defining
which gates will open.

      (each section of a city a fort or reservation)
It has forced people
to walk roads
built on the bones
of their ancestors,
driving them down them
with promises made of fool's gold
or the threat of bullets
made of real lead.

      (when departure is forced, there is always a trail
of tears)
This is America
and it is nothing new
to fall victim
to the sharpened blade of greed
as it cuts through your possibility
like a machete through cane.

      (you really think you own your labor)

This is America
where the poor
push "the hustle"
giving in to the lie of work hard,
where you think you can catch up
to the ones whose children's
children's children eat your salary for breakfast.

(wealth is a thing passed down, and folks who
have it ain't gonna read this poem)

Score

● ● ●

What are you listening to?
That your mouth has stayed closed.
That your hands stay still at your sides.
That your body has not pushed up
from its chair and yelled no
with every inch of skin.

Has the alarm not sounded loudly enough?
To ring in your ears.
To require the amygdala to respond.
To make you decide between fight and flight.

Is the sound of a bullet entering flesh too much of a
sigh?
Is the hiss of tear gas too much of a whisper?
Is the sound of a club beating a bone into breaking,
just a snap in your ear?

What are you listening to?
Is your score
the same as mine?
One meant to accompany a post-apocalyptic film
where the year is one not that far away,
where violins accompanied by timpani
always play the opening bars.

Or has it remained a quiet one?
More meant for romance than revolution.

Toque de Queda (Curfew)

● ● ●

How late
will I be allowed to be
a revolution:
> before they teargas my path home
> before a rubber bullet road is built
> to guide me away
> from the chorus of voices
> I have added mine to

before pellets are fired into my eyes
so that I cannot see

How early will they decide:
> that rubber must turn to metal
> fatal, instead of wounding

> that my body is only of value
> as an example of what will happen
> when you disobey
> when you oppose
> when you wake up
> when you stay past the time they believe
> a revolution should live, on streets
> stained with our bodies

Raga Chandrakauns

● ● ●

open nights,
when the light
of a moon
full in its cycle
reveals a snake in the grass
and your bare feet
drive through the blades
into a midnight dance
made of silences
slide into the insanity
of a music made from waiting

new moon
crescent
half moon
full

open nights
when the mind is lit
into a madness
that a city welcomes
with a skyscraper embrace
while the light of the moon
drives shadows
from corners

moon full
mind full

forced into partnership
know
there is nothing safe
about how light
invades an hour
accustomed to darkness

Ciego

● ● ●

I see, I am dangerous.
I see, I am a threat.
I see, I am change.
I see, I am the people.
I see, I am the one that speaks.
I see, I am the one that knows.
I see, I am the one that will not take it anymore.

I see, so you point your weapon.
I see, so you fire.
I see, so my eyes become your target.
I see, so you make sure that your bullet hits the mark.
I see, so you try to force me into blindness.

I see, 'cause there is no turning a blind eye.
I see, 'cause oppression is the darkness I can't live in.
I see, 'cause when you pointed that gun I saw you.
I see, 'cause when you shot out my eye I saw you.
I see, 'cause you can't blind an uprising.

Sleep

● ● ●

I have learned to sleep on my side,
sleeping on my back brings nightmares.
These nightmares wake with me,
bring visits from men dressed in brown.
Temptation tattooed on their arms, they bounce
their triceps sending messages in plena rhythms
that promise me health. I choose my illness and
they moonwalk away, leave
the smell of mentholated cigarettes in their stead.
My weakened body shivers and I hear
my wife singing hymns
in the kitchen. I sleep.

Beware when the Devil Comes to Visit

● ● ●

Never trust a man in brown
especially when he shows up
at the foot of your bed,

shoes shined, suit pressed,
pants creased, hat tipped,
clean shaven, even.

He'll remind you of the suits
that hang in your closet unused
as he wipes invisible hairs
from the sleeve of his jacket.

Tired, you will be tempted
to accept his invitation
to walk into the closet,

where he has selected
a brown suit for you.

Job on a Stoop

● ● ●

Sitting on a stoop on Chapin Street,
Job sings corridas to God.
Trained voice
needing to empty
into the ears of strangers.
Recounting sins
in whole notes.
Alcohol,
tobacco,
women,
all given up
for Christ.

Satan wants to finish me off,
he says, finger crossing his neck
left to right.
He has taken what I most care for.
It is a test
but I will not lose my faith.
Young wife
ran
taking
family. Faith?

Job references
each moment of his life
with a hymn
dressed in the

rising and falling
of corridas and mariachis.

Job waits for a miracle,
sings his hymns,
asks for prayer.
I need for my lord to embrace me
he says, and wraps
his song scarred arms
around himself.

spanish joe finds his father

● ● ●

it ain't a place we're usually welcome
but flaco frio   fat jesus and i
we go where we feel moved to go
and the girl who works there
what she gonna say

> gonna say   "can i help you"
> gonna say   "is there something you need"

galleries always have something i like
images that call my eye and make me think
but this one had a piece of me i needed
had a piece of me i didn't know existed

an image of *el viejo*
not the man who
> made me
>> broke me

let me know
i had no worth

not the father i battled against
this was the picture of a man
i rarely caught a glimpse of

here i see him
> seeing me for what i am

so i offer to buy him
    so i can watch him watching

pull the wad from my pocket to show i can pay
but the girl who works there, what's she say

    she says   "the artist isn't selling"
    she says   "there is nothing i can do"
    she says   "it isn't for sale"

so i send fat jesus to distract
    'cause in this photo *el viejo* is focused
let him talk her up
    'cause in this photo *el viejo* has nothing bad to
say
tell her she is more beautiful than she is
    'cause in this photo *el viejo* saw beauty in me

let flaco frio watch for her return,
    so that i can watch him watching

i peel this image from the frame and mat
and slide it under my shirt
hugged against my skin

we leave and she ain't none the wiser
just smiling a piropo induced smile
never knowing that this heist
hit the heart hard and softened it
against the old man

who knew my anger
as clearly as he knew his own

Self Portrait in Lee Jeans
and Suede Pumas

● ● ●

there is nothing
to see here

nothing out
of the ordinary

just another passenger
on the downtown bound 5 train

looking for silence
in the rumbling of train, track, and tunnel

searching for anonymity in rush hour crowds
cassette bought and dropped into Walkman

soundtrack sampled

Hiding Place

● ● ●

The doorway to your favorite hiding place
is the Prospect Ave station,
where you hop over the turnstile
when you hear the train coming.

On the platform
place your headphones on your ears,
press play on some house or latin hip-hop,
choose between,
the #2 or the #5
both heading into Manhattan.

Choose the #2 but
do not hide yourself.
There are things you need to say,
things that others need to hear leave your mouth.

When you want to disappear, do it knowing
that when you step off the #2 train heading downtown
and get lost in a crowd of people
who do not notice you because they are lost
in worlds you make up for them,

you need to return
mouth cluttered with words to organize,
eyes crowded with images you will translate
ears composing notes into a song, that you will turn into.

You need to return
to that project apartment

and the brother whose voice is so much louder than
yours,
and the mother whose silence is mirrored in you,
and the father who sings off key, who loves another,
and the sisters who you never quite understood

and let sound fall from your mouth.
Even if it is a wail to let loose the years of holding back
tears,
even if it is a curse, a fuck, or motherfucker, or coño,
even if it is a single word, yell it
with the door of apartment 2A open
standing in the threshold
so it echoes in those empty hallways
and slides under door jambs
to a person who needs to hear it.

Hopping the train

● ● ●

1
turn back the turn –
style and slide past
this method is not recommended
for people with big asses

2
go under
like grandma showed you
when you were past two
but still short enough to
look like you ain't have to pay

3
wait for the train to pull up
watch for cops, clear
grip both sides of the turn-style and hop

4
two bodies one token
the subway spoon

5
the handicap gate,
self-explanatory
be quick as a wheelchair
sliding downhill

Searched

● ● ●

Mornings I stand,
stretching arms out
as if in preparation for flight.

Let strangers' probing hands
roam my body

looking for the anger
I might've stored,
steel sharpened, razor thin.

Looking for the revenge
I might've tucked
into the small of my back.

At fourteen
I am a threat.
Searched daily,
nothing has been found.
The right places haven't been searched.

Hands can't find the bulge
of my depression,
can't slide across
the sharpened edge of my loneliness.

Mornings I stand
stretch my arms out

as if in preparation for flight,
hoping feathers sprout

from my pores
and I take to the air

away from searching hands
and into the arms of a sky
that knows the things I hide.

watching the young'uns hang out

● ● ●

backed by colors
hissed onto brick walls
they sit

jacks lit
smoke
inhale
release

they roll scars
igniting wounds

Tire Them by Flight

● ● ●

He runs.
Malt liquor pours
from the bottle in his hands.

Each drop that hits the ground
transforms the playground he runs on
into a battlefield
the bottle he carries
into a weapon.

He runs.
His eyes search
for a place to make a stand,
someone to stand with him
the courage to stop running.

ain't that a motherfucker

● ● ●

children leave their lives with me
and i play them back like b movies
hoping i can edit out nightmares

recorded in black and white
played on prehistoric filmstrip projectors
these are the stories i try to ignore

but can't, i have a role in them
only one line

i love you

'cause what else can you say
to the boy strapped to the gurney
or to his father
who standing beside you says
i just need to sit with him and pray
then gets in the ambulance
and heads to st. elizabeth's

i love you

'cause you can't replace
a ripped rectum
and even if it heals it is never right
and 300 pounds of uncle

pressing you into a mattress
doesn't ever go away

a letter came from prison today
from a boy who wrote about freedom
i read it over and over again
wishing bullets back into gun
wishing drug drained from blood
writing in reply
i love you
filling 18 pages with it
so that each year
he could read a page full of love

my critics tell me i misrepresent
it isn't all bad, and i agree
so I sift through filmstrip
after filmstrip
placing them into two categories

these are the good times,
and ain't that a motherfucker.

The Priest is a Wolf
and the Bishop is a Lion

● ● ●

There are demons dressed as saints who lay
sinning hands upon unmarked skin, staining it.
They whisper prayers to their lust
in the corners of the church
while they roar condemnations
in the form of scripture from the pulpit.

Y dicen las hermanitas, del Sagrado Corazón:
Muchachas tengan cuidado, que ese obispo es un león.

Men take vows but place the promises
so deep in the throat, they stick there
hidden behind desires they keep disguised
as caring, until they hurt. There is no forgiving
how desire drowns the vows a man takes.
There is no forgiving pain delivered
as a blessing, a force-fed communion
that feeds the damage to the spirit.

Y dicen las hermanitas, del Sagrado Corazón:
Muchachas tengan cuidado, que ese obispo es un león.

Be careful for the priest is a wolf
and the bishop is a lion.
So prey, pray you are not
the body and the blood

pray away the altar and the pew
where you are served up as sacrifice.

Y dicen las hermanitas, del Sagrado Corazón:
Muchachas tengan cuidado, que ese obispo es un león.

Self Portrait in Green Overcoat and Purple Messenger Bag and Chalk Powder

● ● ●

Children notice everything
and you can begin to see

only when you understand this.
You know nothing about yourself

except what nine- and ten-year-olds
point out. Here you are

lost, like language
in the mouths of children

who silence their difference
to keep fists from reminding them.

You fill a chalkboard with ways to respond
teach the words that in their simplicity

become a shield. You aren't the silence
of your own childhood. Voice has become

a thing to be passed down, to be taught
so you find yours.

Separation

● ● ●

There are those who would decide a child's fate
driving them into cages where they wait
for the memory of hands
that held them lovingly to return,
drive away the animal that is separation
the one that hovers, the way only time ever really does.

Santa María, líbranos de todo mal.
Ampáranos Señora, de ese terrible animal.

When cages open, there is a moment
where those held within the wire enclosures
deny the reality of their freedom.
Not because it is not desired, but because
there is no memory of it
and the shadow of imprisonment stands upright
like a bear, blocking all the exits.

Santa María, líbranos de todo mal.
Ampáranos Señora, de ese terrible animal

There is an exorcism that must occur,
a hunt perhaps is the better word.
One where the hunter is armed
with the sharpest of knives, maybe a machete,
that will disembowel the predator, that threatens
the freedom we are always running towards.

The Fingers Dance a Yanvalou

● ● ●

Childrens' voices
play with the simple melodies
the earth taught them.

Ears stuck to wind
they listen for what the waters say,
place their fingers upon the earth
so they can read the vibrations.

Their songs strike the ear drum.
The heart pounds out accompaniment
in duple meter. The fingers
dance a yanvalou.
The eyes close.

Prayer,
is there another synonym for songs
sung by children who put themselves to bed
amongst the rubble of a quaking earth.

Blanket

Tanka for a man who during an earthquake,
sat on a blanket he spread on his lawn and
was spared

● ● ●

When earth feeds its hunger,
opens its hole of a mouth
and swallows meal whole

there is nothing to do but
spread a blanket, imagine

silence and stillness.
Prayer comes slowly in this,
a music rising

from this blanket, island
upon an island, sinking

into a shaking
that cracks my vision of her,
a mother angered,

blinded. Perhaps that is why
she has passed this blanket by.

My eyes are scarred now
by friends swept into the earth,
but hope is in light

that mutes the echoes of screams
and allows for survival

upon a blanket
I will fold, put away,
will to my child.

A child who sat beside me
and lives to wake in light.

Carreta de Muerte

In conversation with *Carreta de Muerte*
by Horacio Valdez

● ● ●

My bow in hand,
I hunt a life
I did not live.

Enough of these things
that are made for the living.

Pick and ax
clear the space,
dig the hole,
bury me a body.

I do not need a horse.
I do not need a mule.
Just this cart,
this place to rest

and a patience
made of bone and hair,
a patience made of time.
Waiting.

I wait. I wait.
I do not need a horse for this.
I do not need a mule.
Just this cart and my hair,

curious thing that will not leave me
a reminder that I was once you,

and you will be me
just bone one day,
waiting in a cart
pick and ax,

no need for a horse,
no need for a mule,
just a cart, where you can sit
and let others admire your hair
while you hunt a life
you want to live.

Matrimonio

In conversation with *The Marriage of the Yachaj and the Uma*, a photo by Karen Miranda Rivadeneira

● ● ●

La Que Une

This is just a role I play,
the task I must complete, this joining.
I am not what you should focus on
that is why the mask on my face
blurs my features. If there is beauty in me
you must ignore it, find it only in the union.

The path is not what you should focus on
that is why stones are scattered along it,
focus on the obstacles.
If there is a direction, ignore it,
learn to make your way
around and over things.

The Proposal

Will you stand in the cold with me?

The Vows

I will stack stones on top of my love
so that it stays grounded
and can't be blown away
like loose snow.

El Que Proteje

I know this union needs protection,
that winds will come to try and tear it apart
I will keep my face as hard as stacked stone
so any threat knows I will be an obstacle
will keep my hand on my machete,
train to use it gloved and ungloved
in the coldest of weather,
so cold will never be a hindrance.

Lotus

In conversation with a photo taken by
Karen Miranda Rivadeneira

● ● ●

"Bodies intertwined are enormous story tellers and in
each embrace a cuento pours out of the flesh."

There is always one
who will carry both shadow and light
who will turn her gaze away from the sun
knowing its presence only by how it warms her legs.

We rest on her as if she were stone
and we were serpent, warming.

Her story stretches
like legs extending in pleasure, released.

There is always one
who serves as transition,
who moves between light and shadow
embracing both.

She understands how light feeds
darkness, how they need to embrace.

Her story drapes itself over another,
protection from the silence of erasure.

There is always one

who will live in shadow,
who will hide behind the light

extend a limb only to be reminded
why she prefers the shadows.

Her story rests on the back
like the black ink of a tattoo,
that if removed would scar.

Together they blossom,
a lotus that carries its stories
in the spaces between
its layered petals.

Le Fleur de L'age

In conversation with a print by Marta
Perez-Garcia

● ● ●

i have discarded the layers of cloth
they dressed me in
not the whore
not the servant
i have donned a finer garment
one made of my own flesh
and the protections that attach themselves
to my appendages and warn
that this nakedness is not an invitation

i was not always this
was made over generations
one transgression at a time,
by the pressure   not the kind to turn
coal to diamond
but one that mutates
brings the snake into my tongue
brings the pistol into my hand

look at how these open eyes
watch my transformation
how I shed skins
and let them fall away
from my body   these eyes take it
all in   let the dreams
sweet or nightmare slip into open mouths

that words refuse to slide from
instead sticking to the back of white teeth

rotting them from the inside out

i have cut through
the hardwood of this frame
let my image stride uncontained
       draw the scent of flowers into my pores
       draw the thorns of roses into my speech
       draw the force of bullets into my fingers
       draw silence from open mouths and turn it
into the song that sings a liberation
from a heavily guarded memory

Sorrow

After Helen Frederick

Have you ever seen yourself
reflected, at the moment
when your sorrow
runs deep as pre-climate change glaciers.
A suffering that penetrates worlds,

when the vast and various burdening
that can no longer be an individual's charge,
becomes a collective's,
forming into surging water
so forceful it clears away the suffering
so sorrow can be cast off.

Santa Lucia

● ● ●

How often
have my eyes
caused you suffering,

the depth of their color
pulling you in,
a dark temptation.

Now plucked
from their sockets
do they tempt?

I set them on this platter
a reminder
that love and faith are blind devotions.

Biblical Erotica

● ● ●

I am not angry at God when I read
from the Song of Solomon. I think of
you and the way my eyes drift
when you undress for bed.
No tienen rumbo fijo,
just wander, teeth, lips, temple.

Biblical erotica uses sheep
and roses to speak of beauty, but I can't
picture these when I look at your breasts,
I think of feeding on dark brown nipples
that I pull honey and milk from. My spouse

I watch and wait for you to come to this
wood, where I am offering you shade
under my apple tree, so that you can
sing me the songs of Solomon's love.

Somewhere Between

After Anna Kodz

● ● ●

There is the body
and what it feels
and what it wants.
And then there is what it is built from,
tiny things
that want only the connection
to other
tiny things

so they can take shape,
become the things we picture,
the things we come to love
become the bodies we desire,
become the bodies we feed
with other bodies.

There is the body,
but what is it
without the tiny things
that when bonded
become the body,
each a unique form
shaped by a million marriages.

Each form will seek out another
looking not at the tiny things
or at the body

but something between
that can connect them,

so they do not try
to tear each other
into the tiny things
they are both made of.

Santa Maria Magdalena

● ● ●

Everybody has to carry their demons
but I carried more than most,
one for every day of the week.

They sat inside me
drawing straws to see who
would take the lead that day.

I had not asked them to leave.
They made my life interesting,
allowing me the liberties of the flesh
and the guiltless pleasures of the possessed.

Then he released me, Jesus:
and I had to find
other forms of entertainment
so I followed him around.

Santos y Diablos

In conversation with a photo by Karen
Miranda Rivadeneira

Sometimes we need to sit with our diablos
let them decide the menu items
to be brought to the table,
let them read the newspaper aloud
and lie about the saintliness of war
and the holiness of hunger.
Let them make it so we need
to bum a cigarette, and light it
with a match, so the smell of sulfur stings
the nose, inhale deeply and let the smoke
burn our lungs so we are reminded
that hell is just another place to meet for a meal.

Sometimes we need to let them stroke our arms
or press their fingers into our shoulders
and whisper shit about the *santos*
que se han colao, disguised
as the diablos they want to be;
the masks just as bright, just as colorful
but just don't sit right on the face,
looking like they are meant to cover something
other than the blemishes collected on the skin
over centuries of sinning.

Don't let the saints fool you
they declined the original invitation

to sit at the table and share in the delicacies
that *la dona de la cocina* cooked on her fogon.

Acted like malcriados, raised without manners
then after remembering the pleasure
in sinning, snuck in through the back door
to sample the things they gave up for sainthood,
realizing we all need some sin in our lives.

The Curandera Guides
the Photographer's Gaze
In conversation with a photo by Karen
Miranda Rivadeneira

● ● ●

The curandera chooses
the moment for you to capture.
Today she chooses to be an object
inside an object, her body an interjection
into the circle of the container she occupies.

She lets you capture her, exposed
her body settled into a tub
like she has settled into her age
her gaze settled
on a moment she will not share.
You do not ask.

She has no problem
with putting her nakedness in your view,
she feels no shame in how she is made,
how time has formed her.

She knows her body
needs to be as clean
as the image you want to produce,
and that once clean she will be able
to determine more clearly
what is dark and what is light
and how to balance them.

Mal de Ojo

*In conversation with Mom curing me from
evil eye* by Karen Miranda Rivadeneira

● ● ●

There is always someone watching
waiting to bring something down on you.
Always someone whose eye
invades the balance between spirit and body.
Someone who will compliment a child
and forget to offer up a blessing,
protection against petty spirits
who want to prove that nothing
is more beautiful than them.

And always someone to block
the path that evil winds down.
Maybe a mother, who knows
the power of crucifixes, el divino niño,
and an egg touched to a body
dressed only in its skin,
curandera who understands the rezos,
los siete jarabes, florida water,
sage, and tobacco,
and practices the rituals
that drive fever from the body,
pushing it to find its way into a glass of water
placed under the bed, or on a nightstand,
where it can no longer heat
flesh into discomfort.

There is always the non-believer,
who does not understand the medicine

of an elder's memory
and its connection
to ancestors who
add their breath
to the smoke, blown
from the lips of descendants
who have learned
how healing is passed down.

Found Poem: Corner of New Hampshire and Piney Branch

● ● ●

Please
> (this is what my mama taught me to say
> before I ask for anything.)

I am need
> (this is my alter ego, my superhero identity
> the one that makes me do this electric boogaloo
> along the double yellow line, that makes me tap
> at your window with this handmade sign.)

Help God bless you
> (cause you know he ain't paying you
> no mind, just like you
> ain't paying me no mind
> but he will if you just pay, a quarter
> a dime or nickel, he'd prefer you pay in dollar bills
> twenties if you have them to spare
> meet me with kindness, in exchange
> blessings, blessings, blessings.)

tia margarita's love affair

● ● ●

tia margarita had a love affair
with laundromats,   she loved
the way the smell of detergent
opened people up to conversation
how the whir of the washers
made people hum their sorrows to her
how the rumble of overloaded dryers
forced her to lean into their stories
and then carry them home
like carefully folded laundry

Self Portrait with Child in Arms

● ● ●

This is the place
where nothing else matters
except how she rests on your chest,
how the weight of her
clears the weight of the day.

I have learned to dance lightly
so that movement
becomes a path to closed eyes.

I have learned to sing plenas
into a silence her cries
no longer interrupt.

I have learned when to:
      warm the bottle,
      change the diaper,
      or just hold her and sway
      as if a salsa song was playing.

Lessons for my Daughter
about Playing Domino

In conversation with *Domino Players* by
Winston Vargas

● ● ●

Aguantala pa' que aprenda

I am the one who wraps himself around you
like a hand around a ficha.

I sit you here so you can learn.
The numbers are not surprises,
there is always an order to them.
Men make the choices
that cause them to seem out of place.

Know that for men at a domino table
a smile may hide a disappointment,
a hand lacking potential
a life, lacking opportunity
and can quickly turn into a threat.

Watch the one who stands behind you,
watch where their eyes land.
You never know what they see
or the message they convey
when they look away.

Heed the warning on the wall
to stop the bullshit,

but know the difference
between that and shit talking.
Let loose the shit talking
so they never know when a capicu
is going to be slammed onto the table.

Buscando un Arbol
Que Me de Sombra

In conversation with *A Hill in the South
Bronx* by Perla de Leon

*Estoy buscando un arbol que me de sombra
Porque el que tengo me lo van a cortar*
Coro de bomba

● ● ●

This building stands,
the last tree to be cut down
in a garden of brick and steel
made desert of rubble and dust.

It still shelters families
whose poverty
bites into them like the rats
that chew holes into their cereal boxes
and gnaw at their toes.

It spits out children to play,
on mattresses evicted by flame and smoke,
then swallows them back in
after streetlights remind mothers
to call for their return.

It provides shade
for the mangy dogs who scavenge
through the leftovers of the leftovers
and then wait below the window

of the woman, who leans out
and like a merenguero playing guiro

scrapes her plates clean
letting each drop of food fall within reach.

Lechón

In conversation with *Lechón / Roasting Pig in
Alley* by Hiram Maristany

● ● ●

Carcass beside a carcass
one of metal, one of flesh
both waiting to be scavenged.

One by men who have become
adept at removing things
that serve no purpose where they sit
and turning them into a working part
and an extra dollar.

The other
by the children who stand
like crows congregating near road kill
to wait for a piece of cuerito
they can peel right off.

Machete en la capota
the hand that grips its hilt
will slice through the flesh and bone
of the roasting animal

or el animal who doesn't understand
the sharp edge of a machete
will cut the guapo out of you

Carcass beside a carcass
proving the dead serve a purpose

and the living will congregate
anywhere the smell of well-seasoned meat
fills the air enough, to house the memory of home.

Even when home is only a story
your mother tells you
while she sits, in a housedress,
hair wrapped around rollers,
feet slipped into chanclas
and planted firmly,
on ground she can't root into
because here only weeds take root
and she is a flamboyan.

Fragmented Still Life

After Soledad Salamé,

● ● ●

There are pieces of this that do not belong,
that have slid into the tiniest of spaces
and pushed cracks into what was,
damaging the topography.

These rivers and hills become
the abandoned buildings of cities,
where rubble is the foliage
of deconstructed beauty.

The wrinkles of age, not grown gracefully
but carved into the flesh of this landscape
cut the color from it
and force the curves into sharp edges.

Hydrant

In conversation with *Hydrant: Hand* and
Hydrant: In the Air by Hiram Maristany

● ● ●

hands gripping wrench pull back
let loose the force of water meant to put out fires
creating a wave
that can be guided with hands or can

and answers the call of children
who feeling the heat of summer
trapped by cinder block walls
and transferred onto their skin
run to la pompa

where force+water+hands
transform gutters into riverbeds
emptying into the mouths of sewers
and crowded with paper boats
floated to see if they could travel
the distance between pump and corner
without capsizing

Self Portrait with Skippies Pulled by their Laces from a Large Bin at Alexander's on 3rd Avenue

● ● ●

"Skippies, they cost a dollar ninety-nine,
Skippies, they make your feet feel fine."

Cruelty is a rhymed couplet
sung by a chorus of voices
that haven't hit puberty yet,
upon eyeing your footwear
and the highwaters that accompany.

But I know that I have two dollars,
75 cents for a slice,
25 cents for a coke,
1 dollar for the penny candy store.

I know my bus pass
will get me home,

where everybody
has the same problems

and the same blessings,
cause there is always dinner,

there is always heat
and the lights are always on.

The Waffle Shop

● ● ●

on the corner of 14th and park
by the payless
thick fingered
salvadoran women
ball up masa

pressing thumbs
into the center
they form a crater
fill it with meat
then pat it into circles

placing it on the griddle
to fill an order
of pupusas revueltas
for the intipuqueño
whose hands are scarred
and calloused
from building homes
for people who pay him poorly
and support the laws
that would send him home
where he belongs

out in front of the waffle shop
a man slowed
by the morning dose of alcohol
grips a metal spoon in one hand

and a paper bag
grease stained and torn
in the other
he sits on the ground
leaning forward
scrapes the spoon
at the steamed rice
he has spilled onto the sidewalk
he tries to salvage a bite
succeeds only in pushing the rice aside

he drags the metal
along the concrete
attempting to dig through
trying to reach
the rich brown earth beneath
an earth he can get in his nails
an earth he can paint his palms
and fingertips with
an earth he can root into
so he can reach out to the waters
of his homeland
and draw them into his body
drowning the need
to forget himself
that this city has filled him with

Keys and Coins

● ● ●

This morning I passed a man by
who asked me for change
though coins crowded my pockets.

At lunchtime I helped pull a man from the gutter
he rolled into, his clothes soaked by melted snow,
body heavy with the dead weight of drunkenness.

When I got home from work I could not open
my door. I'd forgotten my keys
so I sat on ice covered steps to wait.

A man passed by swinging his keys. When
he shoved them in his pocket, I thought
of the coins in mine. Nickels, quarters, dimes
that could not open my door, the seat of my pants
was wet and no one would be home for hours.

Jesus Drives Past Mary Magdelene

● ● ●

Mary walks down 13th street,
her cotton dress
unbuttoned to her waist
exposing her ashy bosom.

She looks into the open eyes
of abandoned row houses.
The shadows call her in
but she still has work to do
before she has enough
to pay for her demons.

Jesus Colón drives to the red light
on the corner of Kenyon.
Watching her come towards him
he rolls down his window.
"Get out the street before you get hit."

Mary turns around slowly
watching the car drive away.
"Jesus," she whispers,
reading the vanity plates.

She moves towards the sidewalk,
and a young couple walks away,
"Like you ain't never done nothing bad.
Oh fuck it, go ahead.
Even Jesus passed me by."

When Dreaming is Passed Down

● ● ●

She is not a dreamer
but dreams come to her
singing their songs,

sometimes off-key and
deafening in their entrance
sometimes, so wonderfully in tune
she wakes weeping.

This is her inheritance,
passed down from mother
to daughter like a name she chooses
to disown, but everyone uses
to call on her spirit.

This lineage of messages
and warnings, of visits
and intrusions keeps her
kicking at the sheets,

keeps her
searching for the meaning;
of a woman in a white room
or a man lighting candles
or a child carrying bones.

Then waking sets her straight
reminds her she is not
a dreamer.

raga lalit

● ● ●

this is the space
where even the birds
are part of the silence

a space
not quite day
not quite night
but sure of purpose

a space
to revisit simplicity
along as many roads
as a song can travel

a space
where the musician listens
for the god within every note
and worships

each repetition
a flower to throw
at a deity's feet
a prayer coaxing blessings
from her

praise

this is the space

where wind and water
sit against each other

and rock   patient
while we grow
around them

the space
where birds arrive
        unhindered

by breath or distance
to listen to the quiet
then sing awakening
in a language
all of babylon will understand

the space their song creates in time
crowded with stories
of wind and water
that arrive unexpected
and drive bodies into shelter

where they watch the skies
and wait for the familiar

hiding from the beauty of a storm
emerging to find themselves
in the rubble of their absence

Visitation

● ● ●

my father walked into my room last night
he must have heard my daughter cry out
and come to see what had bothered her
this is the first time he's come back

he seemed rested
and the laughter that mom missed
was back in his face
i don't remember if my eyes
were open or closed

i called mom to tell her
that papi had come to visit
she told me members of the church had seen him
standing in their doorways
waiting for them to come and pray with him

they see shadows in their homes
and unafraid they greet him
whispering, *mi pastorsito*:
my little pastor.

notes to my father

● ● ●

papi,
mami is troubled
her memory comes
in pieces she can't connect
the spaces sadden her   she feels
she can only keep portions of you
and that those may soon go

i have kept your bibles
i search the notes in the margins
for things i missed   lessons
you wanted me to learn
i'm listening now

papi,
i gave your granddaughter a sketchbook
she fills it with drawings of you
you are always smiling

sometimes the baby cries out   papa
i look for you in the corners of the room
search for the rustle of a curtain

papi,
we've removed the plastic covers
from the sofa cushions
don't worry there are no stains on the fabric
a minister from ecuador is wearing your suits

they say his sermons have become fire

i have not returned to church
i am angry at god

perhaps one day we will reconcile
for now i will address my questions to you

Artifacts

● ● ●

Some things find their way,
others are given their purpose.
You have been down both these roads
and understand that what you represented
is no longer even a memory.

The earth you are buried under
has forgotten you are
present.

Now that you are
no longer of use,
you are dug up.
Hands treat you tenderly,
you are placed
in a corner,
      on a pedestal
           or a mantle,
photographed
and placed in tabletop books
or museum catalogs.

You are written about
in words that switch between
the scientific and the flowery
when really you were just
a thing, nothing

to be praised,
a thing to be bartered for

or sold in the chaos of a market,

and now
a thing detached
from path and purpose.

Sunflowers

● ● ●

In a McDonald's on Brentwood Ave.
an older woman complimented a young man
who had added a polite smile to his service.

When he looked embarrassed she said,
"I want to give you your flowers before you die."

So I stand on the corner in front of a vendor
and watch as he wraps a dozen sunflowers.

These are My Ghosts

● ● ●

These are my ghosts
the ones that haunt my skin.
Can you see the lines they draw

around my eyes? I want
nothing from them but they want
pieces of my five-o'clock shadow
they shave me with their stories.

It's a patchy shave
done on hangover mornings.
Can you see the lines they cut

into my cheeks? They collect
the hair and skin to keep as evidence
they existed, that they are free to do as they please.

I remind them of their crimes,
of how they need to blend into my portrait
that there are posters of them
in phantom post offices
and I can turn them in.

Self Portrait with Fedora
and Button Down

● ● ●

At this point in my life
I should know better.
And maybe I do.
I know sometimes what you say
does not carry what you intended.
That a poem, like a life
can be read a dozen ways,
so watch your line breaks
and your punctuation.
Make decisions
as if they were typewritten,
where every mistake
requires a multi-step process
for correction.

CPSIA information can be obtained
at www.ICGtesting.com
Printed in the USA
JSHW060959281222
35431JS00001B/16